T5-AOA-756

There's No Room (for)...

Lessons I've Learned from My Sister and Am Still Learning

William T. Scott, III

There's No Room (for)...
Lessons I've Learned from My Sister and Am Still Learning
by William T. Scott, III

Copyright © 2020 by William T. Scott, III

All rights reserved.
No part of this publication may be reproduced, stored in a retrieval system or transmitted in any form or by any means, including electronic or mechanical. Photocopying, recording or otherwise reproducing any portion of this work without the prior written permission of the author is prohibited except for brief quotations used in a review.

"My Purpose," words and music by Jill Gallina
Copyright: 2018 GallinaMusic LLC
www.jillandmichaelgallina.com

Book cover and interior designed by Ellie Searl, Publishista®

ISBN-13: 9780578734828
LCCN: 2020914417

T. Cooper Thompson Publishing
Landenberg, PA

Contents

Acknowledgments and Author's Notes 7

Foreword 11

Preamble 13

There's No Room for Unkindness 17

There's No Room for Insecurity 21

There's No Room for Combativeness 27

There's No Room for Poverty 33

There's No Room for Intolerance & Impatience 43

There's No Room for Violence 51

There's No Room for a Lack of Community 59

There's No Room for Mistrust 67

There's No Room for Oppression 73

There's No Room for Hopelessness 79

Epilogue 83

"My Purpose" by Jill Gallina 85

Acknowledgments and Author's Notes

ALL PLACES AND PROPER NAMES are real and times and dates referenced are accurate to the best of the author's recollection. Exceptions are noted prior to the appropriate chapter.

Many of our life-long friends are mentioned in the book, some by name and some not. Omissions of such are not intended, but their often bi-coastal presence in our lives enriches us upon each reunion and each provides inspiration in their own ways, all figuring as those whom we should seek to emulate.

My sister and parents figure prominently in sections of this work and I could not have accomplished this volume without their input and sustained patience with reading multiple versions. Not only do they live by the golden rule, they express the highest degree of acceptance, love and support anyone could imagine.

Lydia and Bill, described in the chapter regarding Community, should deservedly figure more prominently; however, their thoughts and compassion surface unnamed throughout. They are true exemplars of the life lived worth living and always strive to be the best people that they can be, all while displaying such Christian love and devotion.

I owe a huge debt of gratitude to Jill Gallina, composer and author of "My Purpose," the inclusion of which at the end of the book so beautifully resonated for me throughout my first journey through the written word. Her kindness, warmth and trust were amazing gifts from one former stranger to another. Check out her choral works and I hope you may be touched and moved as I was (and still am).

The creative and stylistic elements of THERE'S NO ROOM (FOR) ... could not have been achieved without the wonderful support of Ellie Searl, owner and creator of publishista.com. Her insight, openness and dedication are true measures of a creative partner and proved invaluable.

I would be remiss if I did not lend my thanks, appreciation and undying love for my spouse, Wayne. His patience, analytic thought and positively critical comments lent the full support one might hope for from a spouse. He has my forever affection and caring for my heart truly resides in his.

Foreword

THIS SMALL BOOK, WRITTEN WITH both hopefully pure intent and heart, was inspired by my spouse who always lives the golden rule and by my parents who must have written it.

We live in a time of great discord and divisiveness. It is the author's hope that the bits of wisdom contained herein will inspire the residents of this world to act with just the slightly higher degree of decency, respect and empathy toward one another and that those *in power* may read this tome and be reminded of their commitment to serving the greater good. While lofty and perhaps unrealistic in purpose, this work may inspire those among the *regular of us* to live more purposefully and with a reopened eye to the travails of those amongst whom we walk.

Lastly, there may be many, many other topics that could have been included in this volume. It was the author's task to narrow down those that were selfishly most important, but the hope is that the contents may inspire additional discourse and dialogue about these topics and perhaps another more inspired than I may write additional and meaningful texts.

Preamble

So, you need to learn a little about this author.

I was born and raised on the East Coast. I am the offspring of a kindly couple who dated in high school and who married in the early-1960's. They settled, initially, in my mother's parents' home and then were able to purchase their first property in a neighborhood in the area. While modest, it was a wonderful place to grow up. I recall that my mother returned to the working world, as a medical professional, to provide me a private education at a local private school not far from our home. My parents sacrificed a great deal for me and I remain sincerely appreciative to this day for their commitment to family.

As some late-teenagers do, I rebelled against the conventions of family, tradition and belief and moved West to attend university. I recall my maternal grandmother (Mamar) asking me 'not to do this' but I remained resolute in my drive. This move involved a change in religious beliefs, which greatly aggrieved my family.

Following graduation from university, and still not resolved with my familial fallout, I followed college friends to Southern California. There I gained employment and fell into a life-long career in Human Resources.

Over the years, my parents and I, and extended family, reconciled, and became closer. Following multiple professional opportunities which took us (more on *us* later) from Southern California to San Francisco and then to Connecticut and then back again to California, we decided to move back to the East Coast. The primary driver of this move back home was, in the literal sense, to be close to Mom and Dad and to be able to provide any care that may be needed prospectively. Upon reflection, however, the visceral and more meaningful motivation has turned out to be not only the formerly stated, but an additional result: the establishment of a very different way of life, living in a country setting while being close to family, establishing a home with some land and scenery and *just slowing down*.

So the *more on us later.* I met the love of my existence in 1996 in Los Angeles. Over the next 25 years, we would share each others' griefs and pains, celebrations and successes as well as multiple job changes and relocations. Wayne is the rock of my life, my exemplar, and the hope for my future.

With that brief and hopefully not overly detailed description, I hope that you find some value, if only a snippet, in the words that follow. It is the author's wish that this small book be received with the belief that there is no judgement, there is no effrontery and there is no repercussion intended. It is only with an intent to help this world that this work is written.

As Antoine de St. Exupery wrote in *LE PETIT PRINCE,* "But the eyes are blind. One must look with the heart."

There's No Room for Unkindness

This is my simple religion. There is no need for temples; no need for complicated philosophy. Our own brain, our own heart is our temple; the philosophy is kindness.
- Dalai Lama -

Well, yes, there is.

As I mentioned in the preamble, I was born and raised on the East Coast.

In my youth, there was, and still is, a large shopping mall located in the area. I recall walking through the mall with my mother and father and sister. Oh, wait ... I've not told you yet about Susan, my sister.

Susan was born with Down Syndrome. If you don't know, this is a condition in which a baby is born with an additional chromosome. That chromosome is Chromosome number 21. This causes an inherent short neck, small ears that veer up, almond-shaped eyes, but, most importantly, a reduced cognitive level. Susan has the intellectual capability of a normal four-year-old.

She has been a blessing to our family . . . please read on.

My parents took care of me and Susan for many years. I slightly recall being at our family home and seeing Susan on the floor of our living room, weighing just a few pounds, awaiting open-heart surgery. Following this surgery she flourished and grew into the woman that we know to this day. My parents lovingly cared for Susan for many years until such time that it was clear that she would benefit from being with those with whom she would be better associated . . . those of a similar intellectual level and in an environment with 24 hour care. Susan spends many, many weekends with my parents but we believe that she enjoys her "home" and her three co-habitants.

Back to the mall: I recall that this occurred in the mid-1970's and walking with my family and Susan down the main street of the mall and seeing the openly jeering gestures towards my sister, generally in a negative sense. I remember feeling so angry at a young man who openly pointed at my sister and said something to the effect of, "Mom, look at that!" Being that I was still in my youth, probably no older than 12 or 13, I had not yet learned the art of ignoring that which may offend and I recall turning around and making a disgusted face at that boy.

While the unkindness that that boy displayed was certainly just that, unkind, my response was of equal measure. I remember that my father may have said to just ignore those who are unkind, but I could not let it go in the moment. I should have listened to my father, and years later, those words to ignore the unkindness resonate with me, unless there may be something that I can do about the act. I have no idea what the future held for that young man; I can only hope that he has gained a level of accepting and understanding that transcends what I then perceived to be unknowing and judgmental behavior. As for Susan, she, perhaps, always displays the ideal reaction: that of indifference and no reaction, other than to march along her way to the food court, as she loves all manner of food. Her goal was to put each step in front of the other knowing that she was going towards the end of the mall where the food court is. This speaks to her ability to focus on a certain objective and to not let things take away from that aim. Here, her goal may have just been walking ahead or getting to lunch; who knows? Ultimately, she does not let her shortcomings stop who she is and she always seems to achieve her desire unashamedly and unabashedly.

Our family was active for several years in a local church which espoused moderate beliefs and proffered a mission of openness and acceptance of the individual. I participated in the youth group there and during one of the regular meetings, it was announced that the group would lead the order of worship for an upcoming service. I cannot recall if I were asked, recommended or volunteered to deliver a short message to the congregation; nonetheless, I found myself somewhat reluctantly standing at the podium one Sunday morning in front of a crowded sanctuary. I delivered a brief but what must have been a meaningful message of thanks to the congregation for warmly welcoming my sister into their arms.

Some 40 years later, I often reflect upon the jarring contrast between the experience at that mall and my family's experience of a welcoming group assembled regularly for Sunday services. I try to keep this memory *top of mind* as I witness unkindness around me. While I certainly do not always have the courage (or opportunity) to right an unkind act, gesture or statement, at the very least the remembrance of this childhood experience prompts me to try to treat every interaction with kindness.

As the Dalai Lama said in the quote at the beginning of this chapter, "... our own brain, our own heart is our temple; the philosophy is kindness ..." I often think of Susan and her *innocence of intent* and *reaction* when seeking to reach her desire. I've been most fortunate to have been exposed throughout my life to one who's innate trait is to espouse, just as the Dalai said, kindness.

There's No Room for Insecurity

POWER STRUGGLES ARE COMMON IN society, not just business. One person wants something from someone else, yet that person isn't willing to budge on the issue and just hand it over. In response, that first person may try to exert their own power and authority (perceived or actual) to try and persuade the other person to concede.
(https://www.universalclass.com/articles/business/power-and-politics-within-a-business-organizational.htm; 1999 - 2020)

[This chapter represents an amalgamation of several of my own experiences, both recent and far in the past; as such, I have not identified any specific individual, time or entity here].

Have you ever been in a work setting where it was very clear to you that another's success appeared to be dependent upon your own failure, or at least debasement? I have.

Years ago, I had a boss I thought the world of. He was incredibly bright, commanding and engaging. When I was offered the job, I was *over the top* happy to accept the role as I relished the opportunity to work for and alongside this individual. He was, quite literally, brilliant and I believed that, selfishly, I could learn a lot from him, but that I could also lend my experience and talents to the organization and help it to move forward with its mission.

I had a charge to develop programs to train the overall staff, as I have had in many of my professional roles, and a function that I have always enjoyed, despite lacking any formal training or education of this sort. I researched and developed several programs and eventually launched one to the company. I was quite proud of the accomplishment as it took several months of reviewing materials, writing slides, reworking many sections and working with others to ensure that my proposed content and delivery method would resonate with all team members. I was happy when I saw that the survey results were generally positive and that I may have made a slight impact to the way that the people there interacted and helped to move the business forward.

It was with chagrin that I experienced the following. I had developed several acquaintances at this company with whom

I had developed a level of trust. The training session that I mentioned was offered many times as the staff population was quite large. An attendee at the first session was one of those individuals with whom I had established a professional but friendly relationship and he was meeting with my manager following the session. I asked him for feedback following my facilitation of the training class and he indicated a very positive response and noted that this had been 'one of the better trainings he had attended' since joining the company years ago and further stated that he intended to share this feedback with my boss.

The next day, I asked my manager if he had heard of any reactions or feedback to the session that I had led. Earlier in the day, I had confirmed with my acquaintance that he had shared the positive impressions he had with my manager. My manager told me that he had 'not heard word one' about the training class.

I was crestfallen at hearing this. While one can never really know for certain the interactions and dialogues that occur privately between two others, I still felt that I had been undermined. I eventually moved on from this company as the level of anxiety that I felt on a regular basis, prior to and following this experience, was getting to a level that was adversely affecting my mental and physical well-being.

I learned something from this experience. Gratefully, I think that I learned more about myself than anything. That being: I am inherently insecure in my skills, abilities and knowledge. This insecurity appears all of the time, unfortunately, and results in the need for approval, thankful gestures and acknowledgment. It's true professionally and personally for me. My error in the above was not to have stood my ground, believed in who I am and what I can contribute and being able to aptly display the value that I bring. This all stems from insecurity.

However, the flip-side is why was my work not at least noticed? For the insecure among us, it is that fear of *not* being noticed that scares us and troubles us the most.

I sometimes wonder how my sister, Susan, would have reacted to the same encounter. If I use my imagination, I can see a bright, caring and sensitive woman if she possessed just one less chromosome. Knowing how she is throughout her life, I could imagine her shirking off this experience with a laugh and moving on to the next challenge. I like to believe that the non-judgmental and accepting elements of her current character would have manifested themselves in these types of situations, as they did not for me. Similarly, although perhaps a bit more assertive in approach, my spouse Wayne, I can imagine, would have *taken the bull by the horns* and openly addressed his concerns with that manager. The fortitude that he displays on a daily basis and not only in situations such as I describe, is admirable and he always approaches concerning circumstances with balance and ultimate kindness.

I have to state that there are other forces that either serve to ameliorate or denigrate our self image. Had the former been the case, I may not have felt that politics matter more than substance, that potentially dishonest interactions are more valued than earnest approachability and that a sincere effort to make the place better matters more than a supposed conversation rooted in that which may have been perceived as untrue.

I own this situation and have moved on from this. It's my hope that we may all remember that, as our mothers taught us, honesty is the best policy but that that honesty, particularly feedback, should be delivered with respect, kindness and purity of intent.

My sister is now approaching her mid-50's in age, and lives on well past what in prior decades was going to be a shortened life-expectancy. We are blessed to have her in our lives. It is my belief that she will return to her Creator as innocent, non-judgmental and sweet as when she arrived. I wonder if she were ordained to be born this way so as not to have had to experience the trials and tribulations that we with one less chromosome endure. She lives her life working for a non-profit organization, and at home lays out her magazines in front of her and laughing, at times uproariously, at *Three Stooges* videos. As she has matured, she has become more social and will often stand right in the middle of a family crowd gathered to share holiday occasions, seemingly believing that she is regaling the group with an anecdote or story; as a family, we believe that she is doing just that. Perhaps she is sharing how much she loved the fried chicken nuggets at that mall so many years ago. She is fortunate, I believe, to not even know the word *insecurity* let alone have any inclination to behave in any manner that could be attributed to that word.

There's No Room for Combativeness

"By belittling others we only show how little and shallow we are."
- Abhijit Naskar -
AŞKANJALI: THE SUFI SERMON,
(cited in GoodReads.com, 2020)

IN THIS CHAPTER, I'D like to touch on combative behaviors, specifically degrading and denigrating comments, actions or even subliminal interactions that may cause hurt or pain. In this world, at least in my limited experience, and perhaps not blanketly true everywhere or on a worldwide scale, what I will simply call combative behaviors, seem to be all around us.

At least domestically, and in my experience both personally and professionally, we seem to live in a state of hierarchy; where the wealthiest, most powerful, most influential, most famous and most highly regarded command our attention.

In the professional sector, many organizations and companies are based on a structure of hierarchy. While I've seen this change and evolve over time, as companies began adopting a *flatter* organizational structure and attempted to adopt cultural values centered in qualities like egalitarianism, *all voices are heard* and views expressed meaningful, and buzzwords like trust, respect and mutuality abound, I'm not sure that this is always the reality. Research any company, for the most part, and you'll most likely find a mission statement, core values and professional expectations of behavior.

In the political world, the hierarchical structure is alive and well and readily visible to all. There is a power ladder that certainly exists, and I would imagine that degree of influence and control increases by level or title held.

I believe that many in the entertainment industry, particularly those most visible to the public, wield great influence in word, action and deed as well as, in some cases, fiscal manners. By way of example, witness the philanthropic gestures of many in this industry, most often during a local or national crisis. I know that I for one, when reading or hearing of a gesture of these natures (which may or may not be self-reported, but news always seems to get out), feel an increased sense of respect for the individual (or organization) driving the act. Equally, I simultaneously sometimes think: ". . . really? I believe this individual to be worth XX millions of dollars, could they not afford to do more?" That self-admission is my own reaction, and I am often not proud of my thoughts. I suppose that we should all be grateful for any gesture, large or small, by any and all. (I must note here, prior to proceeding, that I can think of many, many examples of selfless and philanthropic gestures in each of these sectors).

Lastly, and I recognize that there may be many more categories here, I think that societally we live in a world of sometimes visible but at times invisible hierarchy. Think for a moment about the images that we see around us with near-omnipresence: billboards, commercials, magazines, online photos and commentary, and, I am sure many other outlets. Do they not, generally, exhibit the best of the best? That is, it's usually the best looking, most successful or wealthiest are displayed. I know that standards such as these and others have existed always; but, in today's society, that moves and adapts so rapidly, at least I seem bombarded with imagery of this nature. Don't get me wrong; I know that we all witness the exact opposite as well: images of isolation, vast poverty, suffering and pain to name a few. But what I am postulating is that I believe that it is human nature, at least for many of us, to compare or judge ourselves against what become standards. For me personally, I know this to be true. I recognize that each of us is different, so I am simply sharing my own experience. Don't we all wish that we were better looking, had a better physique, were taller, and/or had a different complexion, etc. The list goes on (and on, unfortunately); we struggle with this everyday as we try to remember that being a good person, thinking of the needs of others first and espousing a humble yet confident, demeanor is truly the measure of the person.

I offer a few examples of combative (or demeaning) behavior.

- Think about some of our leaders. Some seem to take any opportunity, using almost any form of communication available, to publicly criticize, insult and demean surrounding persons and organizations.

- Think about the *spats* that happen, often between entertainers, politicians or others. These spats are often published in the media and provide, to many, ungarnered attention. Do we really believe that it is healthy for our children, or any of us, to serve as witness? Should news outlets actually cover these?

- Lastly, think about ourselves. I know many, many, very good people. It's almost human nature to speak or think ill thoughts of another (use your own interpretation of *another* here). I know that I find myself often having feelings or thoughts of disgust or judgment about another. In the worst case, these feelings or thoughts are expressed and I find my conscience telling me to adopt more positivity and to never speak (or think) ill of another. I often fail, but at least the conscience speaks.

Here I cite an example close to my heart: Wayne. While he certainly has his moments of criticism and sometimes directive behavior, he has to be the most accepting individual

There's No Room (for) ...

I know. There is rarely a situation where he may be or feel wronged that he demeans those who may be responsible. In our personal relationships, I am unable to count the number of occurrences where he has either chosen not to mention his feelings, cast judgment or set an expectation. Don't get me wrong: he is not without a strong will and the ability to express his opinion ... just the opposite. But his expression of such is always with the intent to be and to encourage others to be the best, the key theme of this work.

The danger of combativeness lies in my belief that, while this behavior unfortunately becomes more widespread, it drives a *new normal* and in many ways, substantiates and permits the pervasive spread and growth of this behavior. Watching those of influence, of whatever type or category, seems to create acceptance of the behavior; however, sometimes one does witness abhorrence as well. My fear is that the influence invades the core belief system of many of us and that we then begin to believe that demeaning is acceptable. Perhaps idealistic? It's just not.

When we think of what we've all heard about most recently, like the *mob mentality, cancel culture* and even the somewhat unexplainable *Karen culture*, what does this all mean? It's probably human nature to "go along with the group," but I have to wonder, to what ultimate end or result? When we think of what I am calling the "mob mentality" do we not often see an unseemly outcome, like looting? I am in no way suggesting that the initial cause or action was not justified; just the opposite: I suggest that the behavior of some may at times become the (accepted) behavior of others and often may morph into an unintended outcome. I think it's a similar question with the last two examples, "cancel" and "Karen" cultures. What is it truly that drives one to act outside of commonly-accepted norms and to act combatively? Is it the will to be different or the inherent desire to express ones belief that we all have the right of self-expression? Or, is it something more deeply-rooted? Could it be fear? (And I'd ask you to ascribe your own meaning to this powerful word, fear, but I will add a few thoughts). Fear of not being considered individualistic or having courage? Fear of the unknown or a lack of belief in the result of a considered action? Fear of exploring something deeper, like a childhood experience or negative impression of self, often resulting from the unthinking statements or actions of others?

I do not pretend to know, but I often think about this concept as I reflect on how I may react, which is why I find myself often "taking a pause" to consider my next action or word. There have been too many times in my personal and professional life that I have reacted in the moment (which is great most of the time) and had to go back to repair what was most likely an unintended result.

We must all try to espouse a trusting demeanor that is grounded in respect for others. I hope that we all can.

There's No Room for Poverty

In the developed world, our understanding of poverty is often based on what we see in our own country. However, even the poorest among us are in the wealthiest 30% of people worldwide. Impersonal stats are our most common window into life in extreme poverty, but what if we asked those in poverty to help us understand what it is?
- Keith Cobell -
(extollo.org, August 8, 2009)

We live in a world of diversity. Diversity of lifestyles, beliefs and values. Diversity of styles, traditions and accepted behaviors. Diversity of ethnicities, backgrounds and genders as well as sexual orientations. Diversity of economic status, standard of living and financial wealth, or lack thereof.

When we lived in San Francisco, the economic divide was most glaringly obvious, at least in most sectors of that beautiful city. One moment you could be marveling at the majesty of the Golden Gate Bridge and the next you may be confronted by a probably homeless beggar. One moment you could be window shopping at a high-end retailer in Union Square and then turn around to encounter a homeless person or even groups of these individuals clustered around asking for any monetary support. Largely ignored, except, I suspect, by the unknowing tourist, these human beings seem to be left to their own devices to survive. So what happens in these situations, to these individuals in need? I am not sure that any of us can ever know.

I often found myself in a quandary that I am sure many felt: do I, or don't I, share the spare change or dollar bill in my pocket with one or more of these people? I more often than not, and perhaps to my own discredit, ignored these requests, often chalking up my lack of action to my consciouses' reasoning that, "Oh, they're just going to use the money to buy drugs or alcohol." While I would imagine that to be the case in many situations, I can't imagine all are motivated by quite the same alluring addictions.

And, here, a caveat: I must note that the City by the Bay has many, many organizations as well as governmental resources, available to this impoverished community. I just always have wondered if there were enough resources to combat the issue.

When we first moved to San Francisco, we lived in a brand new condominium building just south of Market Street. The condo was lovely and had beautiful views of the city. While sequestered in what by relative terms could be termed luxury, the area was surrounded by the homeless and drug addicts. Of particular note, the corner most adjacent to this building and its cross street was a very busy intersection. The homeless gathered there to beg for spare change, whether from the passing pedestrian or drivers stopped at a red light. Many of these individuals appeared to have lost a limb, limiting their upward mobility. As we walked most places, and had many, many welcome visitors from Southern California and other locations, it was a necessity to pass by these groups. One felt an odd sense of quandary at the number who had lost limbs, combined with a contrasting sense of wanting to help, but further contrasted by the aforementioned (if I did share some spare change, to what ends would those small funds be used?).

Three years later we moved to a different condominium in a converted loft building, although not far away from our fist place, the building to which we moved, was, in a prior life, a then-shuttered warehouse. The building had been converted into amazing lofts, with incredible interiors, high ceilings and amenities, including 24 hour security and a concierge. We were fortunate to purchase a penthouse unit which afforded us the opportunity to have a small upstairs room (used as a guest room and reading nook, which led to a rather expansive private deck offering downtown city views). We invested some funds to improve this area with pavers, a built-in grill and nice outdoor furniture. The views of the city were breathtaking, and were nearly 200 degrees from south to north. The three other neighbors on the penthouse level: one owned hotels and the other two built very successful Internet start-up companies; you would know their names as each garnered great success. My spouse and I often would look at each in wonder: "How did we ever get into this crowd?"

The worst part about this area of town was that it was (and is still) one of the centers of the homeless population. Next door to our building was a shady hotel. A former US mint was just adjacent, and laid, for the most part, vacant, despite the city's attempt to remodel and reopen (I believe funding was the issue in not proceeding). The plaza was home to roaming individuals and groups of people. Some were tourists, anxious to try the coffee served nearby by a locally-famous bean brewery but many more were homeless.

Now I must share an experience about which I am not proud. There was regularly a woman on the plaza begging for money. I recall that one day I was seated in the plaza, enjoying the warmth of the day, and this woman approached a couple, who I assume were tourists. They seemed inclined to give her some spare change. I spoke up and told the tourists to ignore her request: 'can't you see her hair? It's wet and looks just washed. Don't give her a dime.' You can just imagine each

THERE'S NO ROOM (FOR) . . .

parties' response. The couple moved on, but I perceived a bit of judgement of my statement on their faces. I used the word "begging" earlier yet this woman appeared to harass people to make them feel guilty for not giving when it was obvious she had a home and was cared for. The woman unleashed a diatribe of expletives against me and also moved on. I still saw her there on a regular basis, seemingly relatively well-groomed but still begging (and harassing). It was not uncommon for many to have government assistance for housing, food and basic medical coverage and live on the next street (in this example), yet many would still engage in activities like these.

This experience is not one of which I am proud. Not only did I infringe upon others' actions and rights (the couples') but I also insulted one, who despite apparent access to facilities, still appeared to be in need and was likely struggling.

What should have my response been? I ask myself that question often when I reflect upon our time in San Francisco. I vacillate between "I did the right thing" vs. "What on earth was I thinking?" I am sure that I will never know the answer to this question, which I would imagine is regularly in the minds of those in the local government who deal with this issue every single day. In a city whose annual budget is in excess of $12 billion[1], of which $167 million and $240 million was budgeted for homelessness programs (respectively for 2014 and 2016), one would think these funds more than adequate to

---

[1] SFChronicle.com, May 31, 2019

address this concern. However, the funding falls short of the need. Since 2017, the number of homeless in San Francisco proper has increased by 17% to approximately 8,000.[2] One must wonder how is the money spent?

Another anecdote, but upon our re-relocation from the East Coast to San Francisco just 16 months later, we purchased a condominium not far from the one described above; our intention was to utilize this dwelling as a second home, not knowing that we would soon be back in the Bay Area again, full time. This unit was just as nicely remodeled (a former newspaper building) but we were able to afford just a one bedroom, one bath unit with a small den (that last statement seems selfish and ungrateful, which we certainly were not). We spent some funds doing some rearranging and added a Murphy bed to the den in anticipation of many guests from out of town. Despite the small 840 square feet of space, we made it work and welcomed many guests over a few years.

Of note, however, the homelessness problem was even more pronounced in this area. When walking to a destination, it was important to watch your step lest you step on a used needle (which I assume was for the administration of heroin) or also concerning, human waste. The odd thing was and is, that this area, known as "South of Market," is a bustling neighborhood with what was then (and I believe still is) comprised of many emerging technology firms and seemingly

---

[2] sanfrancisco.cbslocal.com, July 5, 2019

There's No Room (for) . . .

constant construction of new luxury condominium towers. Just across the street was a very upscale gym and numerous, well-known restaurants were just a stone's throw away. But you'd regularly encounter the homeless; such a contrast to the throngs of people exiting BART (the Bay Area Rapid Transit system) walking from Main Street to their new and promising, and, in many cases, lucrative, roles at tech firms. The contrast was stark, even more so than our previous experiences.

A co-worker of mine, Richard (the best sales person ever, and a man with a true and giving heart with the highest level of integrity), recently shared a story with me. He and a professional associate were visiting the Bay Area for business. During one of their free evenings, they secured tickets to a concert. While waiting in line, they were approached by numerous homeless individuals. My co-worker related that his associate pulled $200 from his wallet and gave the funds to one of the beggars. Richard shared that he made a statement something to the effect of '. . . are you nuts, he's just going to buy drugs or booze . . .' The associate's response was one of humility and of a giving spirit: '. . . no matter what the use, I may have helped someone in need today . . . and I am blessed in more ways than I could have ever imagined . . .'

I now rarely experience a homeless person. We are now living in a rural area in the Mid-Atlantic region, and we regularly travel to shop for groceries in a relatively well-to-do town. I have seen just one supposed homeless person, standing on an island in the middle of the entry to this shopping center, with a sign asking for "any help that you can give." I broke my own rule and purchased a meal on one occasion for this person from a local restaurant. Perhaps I shouldn't say that I "broke my own rule." I simply recalled our days on the West Coast and felt a longing to right what may (or may not) have been a mis-directed philosophy. I've not seen that person since. There is, perhaps, a difference between sharing a meal and simply giving money. Even though that may not be what that person needs or wants, the gesture satisfies my urge to help.

I hope that many of you as readers of this small book may never experience homelessness, and perhaps somewhat less-importantly, the experiences that I shared above.

Why is it that some in this world have so much, at least monetarily, while so many have so little? We regularly read of entrepreneurs, CEO's, politicians, organizations and celebrities who have such wealth and seem to gain more with each passing close of the stock market. As I mentioned in an earlier chapter, I know that many, many of these individuals, and organizations, espouse and *live* philanthropic efforts. However, one does question why one person needs billions of dollars. I often reflect upon our experiences in San Francisco and wonder if just one of these billionaires were to offer several millions of dollars (which I would imagine is a fraction of their overall worth, given the budgetary figures referenced above) to the City, could homelessness be eradicated?

I often attended Sunday worship service at a local Church in San Francisco. The service was very non-traditional, composed mostly of music, sung by a huge and talented choir with very gifted soloists, but there was always a message of hope and inspiration as part of the hour. This organization was much more than simply a place of worship, and, while it attracted a wide and diverse congregation during two Sunday services (many of whom I perceived to be homeless or in need), it also provided a food bank and daily meals to anyone needing assistance (with no proof of need required). They also provided many other services, all free of charge. The facility was not glamorous or ostentatious, lending to its sense of a priority to serve the community. This was a place where I felt a connection to the broader community, the presence of something more powerful than I and a solid commitment and desire to make a difference.

This organization also gave out bags of groceries on a regular basis, and the traditional holidays were no exception. I would walk home after attending a service and the most direct route involved passing through the edge of the Civic Center area of the City. I would often see, and most obviously during the holidays, people with their foodstuffs splayed out on the sidewalk, seeking to sell the bag of generic rice or off-brand can of beans. I am not proud of my (internal) reaction, one of disgust and judgment, fully believing (and probably rightly so) that the items were part of the bagged groceries provided free of charge by this organization. As I reflect further on this experience, how could I have ever known the circumstances facing these people, but I still reacted. I even wondered why the organization had not put a stop to this, even recalling that when I volunteered there with work once that I would swear that I had seen several of the same people come back through the line a second time. I found myself compounding upon my earlier sentiment of wondering if I should or should not be more philanthropic in my approach and belief. I suppose it may be idealistic to think that it is best to give no matter what the ultimate use of our gift may be, but that is really hard for me to do.

When we look around the globe, we see images of wealth, the middle class and those who are impoverished. Could we not, whether by legislative action, corporate giving, individual sharing (at whatever level) make more of a difference? I chide myself for not espousing more of a gracious and giving demeanor in a few of the experiences I shared in this chapter, but I hope that I, as one single person, can remember that it's more important to give than to receive, no matter what the circumstance.

There's No Room for Intolerance & Impatience

With all lowliness and meekness, with longsuffering,
forbearing
one another in love.
- Ephesians 4:2, King James Version -

EARLY IN MY LIFE, NEAR or around the same time as the experience shared in the first chapter with some credulity and judgement expressed towards my sister, Susan, I experienced an example of intolerance. It must have been just around this time, as my maturity level, and attendant response, mirrored that which I described in that first chapter.

At the same local mall, my family and I were shopping, for what I cannot recall. I remember seeing a couple walking our way from the opposite direction. I noticed that the couple was affectionate and holding hands, rather young, and, most pointedly, of different ethnicities. I recall that the man was Caucasian and that the woman was African American. I must confess that, at this point in my young life, during the mid-1970s, I did ponder this then remarkable association: a couple of mixed race. I found myself questioning this in multiple manners: moral, religious, philosophical and practical. I cannot recall specifically, but I believe that I stared in somewhat of a state of disbelief, as it was not a common-day occurrence back then. Hence, my reflection to my reactions related in the first chapter.

As in the case of the reaction to my sister, I turned around and noted several physical acts and reactions of disdain, including an older couple's repugnant facial expressions, another family's actual physical move away to avoid coming in close contact with this couple, and, somewhat to my surprise, a mall security employee seeming to lag behind but, in my view, clearly following this couple.

I cannot recall exactly, but I believe that I asked my parents about this. I am reaching here, but I would imagine (and slightly remember) that their reaction was one of kindness, tolerance and the importance of espousing an openness to the very personal choices of others in the world.

There's No Room (for) . . .

When I reflect upon this experience, and, albeit this occurred probably during the 1970s, I now feel a sense of pride for this couple, even though I have no idea who they are, where they may be now, or what fate their future held. I only know that now I feel a deep and visceral pride in the courage that it must have taken for that couple to appear in public, in that age, and display their love (or certainly "like"), in that environment. I remain somewhat ashamed of my reaction, and I can easily chalk that up to *the times at hand* and my age, but that would be cowardly. More profoundly, perhaps, I should feel a sense of gratitude that my attitudes now are more informed and tolerant, but far from perfect. At the end of the day, and wherever this couple may (or may not) be, I salute their courage, affection and daring to express their true feelings in the face of potential adversity.

In our world of today, we regularly experience intolerance. Witness the myriad protests, usually race- or politically-based, and sometimes involving an encounter with law authority (and, unfortunately, at times, the needless destruction of businesses, personal property and human life). Is it not a moral sadness and shame that the activities of some groups or individuals resort to this level? What must drive the thoughts and actions of these persons? My simple postulation is intolerance. While I and many others, I am sure, support the importance and right of personal expression, I have to wonder if those rights extend to the actions resulting in some of the outcomes referenced above. If we, as individuals, thought of the diversity and values of others, could care just a bit more about the importance of individual expression and beliefs, could this world not be a bit of a better place? I am not at all espousing a view founded in either irresponsibility or idealism; rather, I am suggesting that it would be amazing if we all just *took a pause* before acting, recalled our own values and morals and acted to support the right way to finding justice. And, I am in no way suggesting that the right of personal expression is not just that . . . a right. I believe that it is the resulting actions that cause the most damage.

I believe that there is another type of intolerance, that of impatience. How often do we encounter people who express disdain at what may be perceived as one acting in a slower, or more thoughtful, manner than what that person desires? I seem to see this personally all the time. Whether at the grocery store, sitting in the queue at the ATM (where I bank, one uses the ATM from the car) or upon waiting to enter an event or a place of interest (define this as you like: amusement park, public garden, movie theater or restaurant, etc.).

Just a few weeks ago, I was driving from the grocery store to our home. As I had noticed on the way to the store that there were several areas along my regular route that were under construction, and it was all *stop and go* through that area, I decided to take an alternate route home. This route was via a more major thoroughfare and spread to two lanes at the top of a hill, with the second lane designed as an entry into a neighborhood. I was driving at or near the posted speed limit of 50 miles per hour, and then I glanced in my rear-view mirror. A white car was very quickly approaching my vehicle from behind. I increased my speed, thinking that this action would assuage what I believed to be the driver's hurry to reach his destination. The vehicle literally tailed me and then moved into the right-hand lane to turn into said neighborhood. I glanced to my right and I recognized the driver to be a person of age, and, as he turned into the neighborhood, I received the (now typical) gesture of expletive, the middle finger. My reaction was of a varied nature. I felt immediately saddened; saddened that I may have caused another individual to react in that manner, saddened that I had this experience (which somewhat still haunts me, hence its inclusion here) and saddened that this caused me such angst. My thoughts varied from wanting to buy a fake kid's sheriff badge and being able to flash it at the driver to wishing that I had pulled in behind the driver and photographed the license plate. I have no idea what I may have done with the number, as I cannot contemplate if the authorities act on such minor occurrences. Still, the entire experience saddened me, to the point that I felt some degree of empathy for this driver and the anger that must have possessed his inner being. Simple impatience or is this intolerance? I have no way of knowing. Perhaps this individual was rushing home to handle an emergency or a situation requiring immediate attention. Likewise, could the perceived impatience have been a frustration with missing a program or event on TV? We all, I'd imagine, have these feelings of impatience (or intolerance) all the time; I find that there are times that I don't even recognize my feelings as either.

My parents shared a story with me, actually not too long ago. Being active members of a Presbyterian congregation, they attended a regular Bible-study meeting. During one of these meetings, a particular verse was being discussed and seemed to cause some level of disagreement and controversy among the attendees. The verse dealt with human sexuality and the direction to "stone" those who engage in a certain behavior. While many in today's era would ascribe the verse to being taken out of context, this was not the case with at least one of the attendees. My father recounted that an argument ensued, as he espoused an opposing view to the direct interpretation of the verse and the expressions of the other group member. While I certainly feel a sense of pride in the statements and actions of my Dad, I have to contemplate if the actions of both parties were of an intolerant, and by either view and measure, justified in nature? I intend no judgment of either party, but both reactions were intolerant in different ways: one the intolerance of misunderstanding and perhaps upbringing the other of passion and conscious belief in what is believed to be right. Can interpretation be perceived as intolerant? Or is it the resulting action or effect that ultimately matter? Generally, we as humans have our own beliefs and for me it may come down to a matter of empathy, tone and respect of others. I share the above example solely to provoke thought; we all cannot think alike and there needs to be room for differences of opinion - there's no room for *it's only my way*. Rather, <u>there is room</u> for individual interpretation, self-reflection and growth.

So who, or what entity, is culpable for these actions and behaviors? I think that it is no one and everyone. Each of us has a human responsibility to treat one another with respect, patience and thoughtfulness. I am far from reaching that goal, given my thoughts surrounding this incident, but I try to be better. I hold the door for those coming behind me, I wave to those who wait at our nearby one-lane bridge for me to pass and I try to express gratitude for any service or gesture that is provided to me, of whatever nature. I wonder what drives the behavior of disrespect, anger and aggressiveness. Is it the exemplars who lead us? Our politicians, television personalities and characters, or some other force? Accepted actions and behaviors are learned by example. I have to think that the actions of those in positions of power *trickle down* to the rest of us and, whether obvious or subliminal, lead some of us to believe that our negativity, or intolerance, is the accepted norm of the day. I certainly hope not.

I try to remain committed to a life that affords a philosophy of tolerance and patience. I'm not sure which is more challenging. Impatience seems to be a more commonly experienced issue, at least for me, while intolerance requires more introspection. We all have our own personal values, beliefs and judgements, but I hope that we may all just slow down a bit, recognize that we are all struggling to survive and better our situations in this existence and that we can recognize the value of every person, each interaction and all connections in which we find value.

THERE'S NO ROOM FOR VIOLENCE

Violence is a reflection of lower, instinctive consciousness—fear, anger, greed, jealousy and hate--based in the mentality of separateness and unconnectedness, of good and bad, winners and losers, mine and yours.
- Aum Namah Sivaya -
(https://www.hinduismtoday.com/modules/smartsection/item.php?itemid=3578)

WHY IS IT THAT THE media is overrun with stories of a violent nature? We see regular news stories demonstrating murder, theft, domestic violence, hate crimes, and on and on. It's been reported that one of the most unhealthy things that we can do is watch the news prior to retiring; we live in a time of relative peace and prosperity, so why does the news media tend to show us something quite different many times? While I understand and support the importance of reporting the news to the general public, I also question why there is so much violence in the world today. I suppose that violence has always existed throughout history, but it does concern me that we are witness to so many stories and images of violence in this age.

One must ask oneself what may be the causes of the rage, virulence and innate anger that drives an individual to commit a violent act. Was it of a genetic nature? Was it a result of ones' surroundings and shared belief systems during youth, or the influence of peers with whom we were associated? I suppose that we will never know the real cause.

While I do not own a firearm, I sincerely respect those who do and I honor the Second Amendment, passed by the legislature in 1798, which honors the right of individual citizens to bear arms. Today, we are witnessing nationwide protests in support of an individual who was allegedly innocent but still killed by a member (or members) of an organization whose mission it is to support and protect us. The subsequent protests have resulted in the destruction of property, loss of innocent lives and civil unrest. A caveat: I am not at all suggesting that we as humans do not have the right to express our views, even in protest.

When we lived in San Francisco, we would sometimes read of hate crimes committed against those who, I would imagine, espouse a different lifestyle or beliefs from those of their attacker. Some of these encounters resulted in minor or major injuries, and, in the worst case, death. I find it quite contradictory that some among us express our right to live and believe as we choose but then find it acceptable to take such actions against those who may be different from ourselves.

Now to the question of war. We all learned our history of the many, many wars and various skirmishes that have happened across this world. When we think of senseless destruction, of property, land and humanity, all outcomes of these unfortunate war efforts, it should aggrieve us that there may be no solution. Politics, social change and economic conditions often fuel the alleged need for military aggression. While I can imagine that many of the concerns associated with each of these three broad areas are quite legitimate (and I am sure that there are many more categories into which one could place the basis for war), could these concerns not be resolved without violence? Why is it that the efforts associated with diplomatic relations, governmental representatives and the general public do not prove effectual in most instances? I propose the following: there is a general human need to be superior. We hear all of the time about our country being the most powerful nation on the planet. Why is that concept even of import? Might we not all be more proud to say that our nation is the most caring, giving and supportive country? Or, a peace-driven and humanitarian place to live? I am not sure if there ever will be an answer, but I despise the idea of war. While I am not a pacifist, and am not suggesting that our nation should espouse that notion, I wonder about the value of the overall outcome of war and violence. Have we truly been better served, as a people, to count our warlike efforts as victories, particularly when one contrasts the victories with the costs associated with these efforts?

Why is there such individually-induced violence? I spoke of this question at the beginning of this chapter, but I'd like to dig a bit deeper. When we hear of unfortunate instances of domestic abuse, a violent, direct act against another or groups (for whatever reason) and often larger actions of individuals coming together to perpetrate violent acts, what could be the reason? I am not sure that we will ever know the answer. Each of us is unique. We all come from a variety of backgrounds, belief systems, cultures, etc. Our diversity as a national community is what makes us interesting, strong and powerful. When turned on its side, these concepts often, and unfortunately, fuel some acts of violence.

Consider the spouse-abusing individual in a coupled relationship. What anger must have been bred in these individuals during formative years? What would ever possess one, whose purported love and devotion to their partner, may drive an aggressive or violent action? Is it the will to dominate? The will to diminish the value of another human's existence? Or the will to quell some level of internalized self-loathing that may be believed to ameliorate that person's own view of self.

Consider further the action of hate, for whatever reason you may ascribe. Whether against an ideology, a religious belief, or a lifestyle, how can others feel that it is justified to physically violate others? Is the cause associated to those with whom we congregate and perhaps share (or influence others to share) beliefs that spur these actions? Is the cause a feeling of threat to the perpetrator's own beliefs? Is the cause more external, as in the influence of the media, leaders or those with the power to influence and, thereby, and by extension, fuel the cause of such behavior?

We all know the history of this country, from racially-motivated oppression like slavery and the senseless murder of individuals of color (or whatever demographic) to the experiences we see in the present day: regular murders for senseless reasons of gain or anger, rioting and pillaging of personal property and businesses that have otherwise no culpability, and random acts of destruction, desecration and theft. Consider the acts of violence of the recent past against those of the Jewish faith and their places of worship. What selfish beliefs drove those who committed violent acts to commit them? Is it the fear of difference? The fear of oppression believed to be potentially caused by this group or the learned denial to accept those who may have a different belief system or values from our own? I do not know the answer.

I will do my best to suppress the feelings or inclinations of violence that I sometimes feel (reference my thoughts about the driver who displayed an unwelcome and unwarranted physical expletive from an earlier chapter - I am ashamed to admit that I did feel a small inclination to cause some harm to this person or the vehicle). Thankfully, I did not act upon that urge. I try to espouse a balance of understanding and abhorrence when I see violence happening either proximally or across the globe. I am realistic enough to know that some acts may be rooted in things that I do not understand, whether justified or not. I try to quell any sense of violent inclination on my part, whether it is screaming at a spouse for the mess left in the kitchen, the shopper taking up the entire aisle at the grocery store while pondering which potato chip to purchase or the impatient person behind me at my bank's ATM. I mention the above with no intention of self-aggrandizement or to trumpet my values. I only relate my personal feelings to bring what I would imagine many of us feel in these situations to light. There is no judgement, and perhaps this is the most idealistic statement I make, but can we not all try, in our own ways, to quell violence (or thoughts thereof) in our society?

Lastly, I think of Susan. The most "violent" behavior that I can recall observing by her was a facial expression: a pout. My paternal grandmother, another "Mamar," raised her own tomatoes and assorted other vegetables. I fondly recall my father and me picking fresh-grown scallions right from the earth, quickly washing them off and dipping them in salt and eating them immediately. I love them to this day, and will often find very large ones at a local farmers market. Susan loves tomatoes (or almost any fruit or vegetable) and Mamar would leave her just-picked tomatoes to ripen on a windowsill in her kitchen. Given that there was a counter and cupboard just in front of the window, one would believe that someone short in stature, as Susan has always been, could never reach the delicious fruit reddening further in the afternoon sun. But Susan could. I can hear Mamar screaming out (a rare occurrence) at finding Susan standing in the middle of the kitchen, tomato juice and seeds dripping from her mouth and the juice staining her shirt, with all manner of detritus on the floor. Upon receiving this light scolding, Susan would pout and stomp away. I have to wonder if her love of food drove her act of perceived thievery or if she held some secret and never-to-be-known delight in vexing her grandmother. If we all could just pout and stomp away when we feel any inclination towards violence I have to believe the world would be just a little bit of a better place.

There's No Room for a Lack of Community

Rav Assi, when he was dying, his nephew entered and found him crying. He said to him, "Why are you crying? Is there any Torah that you did not study and teach to others? Look—your students sit before you. Are there any acts of lovingkindness that you did not do? Furthermore, despite your stature, [you humbled yourself and] you stayed far from disputes and did not allow yourself to be appointed over the affairs of the community."
- Rabbi Jill Jacobs -
(The Importance of the Community [Kehilla] in Judaism, jewishlearning.com)

It was years after my college days that I ever regularly attended church. I mentioned earlier in this work my occasional presence at a church in San Francisco, and we did attend services, on a regular basis for some time, in Los Angeles (at a small local church, with a welcoming and warm congregation).

It was nearly three years after we moved back to the East Coast that we began to seek a community of faith with which we could be associated, feel as if we could make a contribution, and feel welcomed.

I must admit that I was rather trepidatious as Wayne awoke one Sunday morning and said that he was going to church. I slept in, albeit alone. For two weeks I stood my ground and slept in on Sunday morning. I suppose that this feeling of trepidation on my part could be attributed to a somewhat rational but, as it turned out, irrational fear of *being different* from those around us (here I am tempted to say "we" but I need to share that my spouse is probably the most accepting and non-judgmental person I know, and therefore, harbors few if any of the suspicions I have). It was on the third week that I attended services at this church.

A bit about this church: we live in a rather rural area, and the church is quite small. On a regular Sunday, there are perhaps between 35 and 50 congregants. That being said, the service is always meaningful and follows the traditional cadence of worship for the religion. I continued to attend on a regular basis, when work did not interfere, and found that I had joined a welcoming, warm and giving community. The small group there each Sunday regularly hugged one another, chatted about local happenings prior to services, and cared for each other in ways that I cannot begin to express.

While I still continue to question, to my own discredit, the existence of many of the elements of this faith (as I suppose it is just that: faith that leads many of us to embrace a belief system), I have found such personal value in joining this community.

There is one couple who stand out as integral to the community, Lydia and Bill (there are many others who have expressed kindness and welcoming to us as well, but I wish to highlight a specific example). We were immediately greeted by this couple in the sanctuary and, over time, a relationship of love, caring and mutual respect evolved. Lydia and Bill, I believe, are life-long members of this faith community, and met in school. Their home is close to ours, so I pass there on most days. I sometimes see Lydia gardening and toot my horn in greeting, always met in response with a warm wave. We have shared many home-baked goods with them and they have always expressed sincere appreciation. They have returned our gifts in greater ways, whether tangible (an amazing, hand-crafted cheese board followed by another unique woodwork, a custom cutting board), supportive (one can always count upon a kind and encouraging word from both) or spiritual (they inspire me each day to live a life of acceptance, love and faithfulness).

Bill and Lydia are exemplars of a life of positivity, gratitude and grace. While I can only imagine what horrors Bill may have faced during the war, and what challenges Lydia may have encountered during this time, we hold them in high regard. I know that Lydia regularly spends her early mornings in quiet contemplation of the wonders about her, the blessings that she experiences and the good will of the Lord.

And Lydia is a true blessing to our lives. Her spirit, tenacity and true humility and grace are examples for us (and I would wish for us all). This couple sustains this faith organization in ways that cannot be measured. Whether it is overseeing the bi-annual chicken barbecue sales, maintaining the church facility, or leading a men's group coffee hour, their commitment and devotion tower above to what many of us aspire.

Speaking of community, I have none, other than the one described above and the very good associations with those at my work. I have struggled to find my place, at least outwardly, here on the East Coast. I find that I am a member of all communities and, counterintuitively, a member of few or none. I find myself (and ourselves) primarily socializing with those few remaining friends from two prior jobs here, my (very important) family, each other, and few others. We have welcomed, and hope to continue to welcome, dear friends from Southern California and San Francisco. These relationships seem to have spanned time, often decades, tribulation and distance. We crave these interactions as they serve to provide a welcome distraction not only from a relatively solitary existence (as a couple) but also the opportunity to welcome others to our home which we selfishly believe to be a place of peace, beauty and warmth.

I wrestle with the concept described in the above paragraph. Meaning, I very much value our home, our lifestyle, our personal associations, our family and friends and the *slowing down* that I described in the preamble. I value the time that we, as partners, have together, even if we get on each other's nerves many times, as couples do. That being said, I often wonder if my efforts should be extended to more meaningful endeavors: volunteerism, venturing out more often or attempting to develop new relationships. I must admit that I am not good at that . . . making new friends. I tend to be one who values an "inner circle" of friends and family, and I seem, for the most part, contented with that approach. However, there are times that I long for a broader sense of community. I am not sure what that may look like, but I would imagine it would comprise a broader sphere of friends, more activities external to our home, or ventures to places yet to explore. I am blessed in that *we have what we have* and we remain very comfortable living our lives in the way that we currently do.

My mind drifts, as often is the case (gratefully), to my sister. What community does she have or belong to? One could argue that she is a member of a familial community at her group home, filled with a life of regular outings and activities, daily trips to work and celebrations of birth and holidays. One could also argue that she is a member of our family, and this would, of course, be true. She is not always present among us, but her *presence* is often felt, and when not in person, missed. Susan also counts herself among several external communities: her bowling team, her *boules* (Bacchi) league, and the annual special needs prom, always accompanied by my mother, but where she enjoys dancing and her style of camaraderie with all those around her, but especially with those with whom I believe her to be most comfortable (as we all are, I suppose): those who are just like her.

What can we learn from Susan? For me, I have learned that community can be nothing or everything. Nothing in that each of us has the capacity to be at peace with ourselves. Should we not be accepting of how we were born, what we believe and how we pass our days? I am someone, amongst many others, I can imagine, who is not always comfortable in solitude. Does this stem from some external force? Of course, community can also be everything. As humans, we tend to gravitate to those of like mind, shared beliefs and values and commonality of thought. There is indeed power in our personal association with others, whether outward or intrinsic.

For Susan, I have to wonder if she really cares one way or the other as to whether she is part of communities or not. I see her being perfectly happy on her own, and she has been known to eschew various gestures of inclusion, even to the chagrin of family when she seemingly ignores an invitation to join for a weekend or a gathering. She's regularly heard to say "home" when she is with others, my parents included, referring to her desire to return to the place we believe her to be most comfortable, indeed her "home." However, by equal measure, Susan visibly delights in the company around her and usually ends up being the center of attention, at least in her own psyche. Wait! I then must alter my thoughts - Susan values community, however we define that term, and those around her. She just values solitude, doing things her way and enjoying her chosen activities undisturbed. I know that I aspire to achieve such a balance of the blessing of community, whether that of self or resulting from association with others.

Susan has taught me that she may be strong-willed, but that she loves those around her ... her communities. She loves her family, co-habitants and friends.

What may be our obligations to "community?" I think that if we are to be a part of a community, we need to be invested. Does this mean helping to create the sustainability of the community? Does this mean contributing effort, thought or time? I ask myself how can I help to ensure that the community continues to thrive while being open to those who may be different from me. This is particularly true of our experience in getting to know Bill and Lydia. The four of us could not be more different in many ways, but there are so many commonalities that are of a visceral benefit to us both.

May you find the blessings that I have experienced, the associations that have existed and developed for me, and feel a part of a community, that, is in most instances, bigger than ourselves. It is with humility that I write this chapter in the hopes that you may find it just that: a gesture of humble gratitude for what we have, a thankfulness for those around us and a gratefulness for each day that we experience.

There's No Room for Mistrust

*Let the morning bring me word of your unfailing love,
for I have put my trust in you. Show me the way I
should go, for to you I entrust my life.*
- Psalm143:8, King James Version -
(https://dailyverses.net/trust)

Have you ever felt that you did not trust what you were hearing? Have you ever felt that you did not trust what you were seeing? Have you ever felt that you could not trust the seemingly innocent or generous act of another? Well, I have and I would imagine that many of us have, too.

In our world of today, we witness myriads of examples of inaccuracies (at the best) and blatant lies (at the worst). Consider the often-conflicting representations of the goings on in the nation and locally that are posited by local media outlets. While driving during my usual errands and commute to work, I listen to two local radio news stations. One of these stations seems to report the objective truth of an event or situation occurring at the time. The other, while often mirroring the reporting of the first station, seems to espouse a different point of view, at least when describing their (I presume) assumptive and causative reasons for the situation or event. I regularly toggle between these two stations, primarily to hope to observe the different "spins" that I described. I am not sure why this activity fascinates me but perhaps it's just interest in the variance of reporting "styles" or a cure for some level of boredom with often driving the same routes, day in and day out. I often wonder what outlet to believe (or trust).

Consider the televised media and vastly different reporting that one can view on various news outlets. I perceive that the often widely dissimilar expressions may be, ultimately, driven by a strategic programming direction to speak to the respective audiences of these outlets and to command their continuing attention. Visit the respective websites of just two of these allegedly opposing news venues and you will see the contrasts in reporting more blatantly. I have often found that reading a text vs. viewing the programs themselves appears to be more revealing (at least for me). I wonder why these organizations may find it so difficult to align reporting to reality and truth. Is it a perceived or actual alliance to an organization, business or political affiliation or (as I choose not to believe, and idealistically hope to be the case) a more altruistic interest in fair and honest reporting? I suppose that we, as members of the general public, may never know the true answer to this question, but we must decide which we believe.

Regarding the act of witnessing a lack of trust, how many of us have seen theft occurring right before our eyes? I am not speaking of the activities related to social injustice (rioting and looting) or large demonstrations of theft and destruction of business or personal property. Rather, I am speaking of the small, individual events. I've been in numerous situations where I have wondered if I am witnessing theft, primarily in the form of shoplifting. I recall being at a large, well-known retail establishment (at the mall I described in the first chapter) and witnessing what was a young gentleman entering a fitting room to try on a pair of jeans. While I was not actively observing this person, and as I was spending some bit of time browsing shirts in the area, I did note that this individual exited the fitting room appearing, in my limited view and impression, to be larger in the lower portion of his body than when entering. Of this I cannot be sure, but this experience spiked my curiosity and when I believed that I was out of sight of this person, I checked each of the fitting rooms and discovered that no jeans had been left behind. Again, I cannot confirm that an act of theft occurred, but I suspected as much. My thoughts then ranged from *should I just ignore this and move on* to *I need to report this to an employee for further investigation*, and all manner of variance of thought in between these two extremities of philosophical questioning. Therefore, and I will never be sure if this were the correct response, I did nothing. Imagine my thoughts, chagrin and crestfallen reaction when I left the mall to drive home. I saw this individual, apparently sitting partially in the backseat of his car removing an outer garment, revealing the jeans closest to his person. I believe that we, as humans, possess an innate desire to *right the wrong*, but in this situation I was paralyzed, perhaps out of fear for my own safety or simply ignorance.

This example may not seem to be directly related to the concept of not trusting. However, I believe that serving as witness to this type of purported action erodes our ability to trust all that is occurring around us. I believe that we develop shields, most often cognitive in nature, that then lead us to a means of thinking and belief that we cannot trust.

What about trusting those around us? Some of us may not be the most trusting people inhabiting this planet but some of us just may be inherently trusting. Should we not be able to enter each and every encounter without filters that limit trust?

Why is it that we as a society cannot trust more freely and openly? I will offer a few possible rationales.

Are we so influenced by the occurrences in the world that we believe that we cannot trust what we are told, what we hear or what we see? Are we so consumed with *self* that it is nearly impossible to feel empathy for another's beliefs, values, statements or actions? Or are we so obsessed with being better than those around us that we must act, with whatever consequence, to do what we can to elevate ourselves above another? Are the things that we heard as children ("... don't talk to strangers..." or "... let me check that candy before you eat it...") so ingrained that it forms who we are as adults? Is this always a bad thing, to not trust? People are often swindled out of money by those of a questionable character—Ponzi schemes and other supposed legitimate deals. It may not be wise to always trust, at least at this moment in time.

I have attempted to relate a few examples of what may actually drive a lack of trust vs. examples of mistrust directly. I try each day to espouse a trusting demeanor, I often fail, but I continue on. I believe that we must all do this too, knowing that the outcome will not always be in our favor, but that the effort to do so is more than worth the result.

Finally, another thought about Susan. Susan trusts all around her: she trusts those who feed and care for her, those who clothe, bath and shop for her and those in the public, perhaps at times to her own disservice and often to my parents' unease and concern. I confess that I admire this trait, apparently inherent to her being, given her condition.

I like to think that Susan benefits from the innocence of demeanor with which she was born. Her perspectives, actions and words have not been impacted during her life as perhaps yours or mine have. She developed into a teenager and then an adult only exposed to family, class- and work-mates and her caregivers (and, of course, the public, but perhaps on a less-regular basis). I can tell that the things that have most impacted her are indeed external to Susan; things like children's music videos, big band music (think "The Lawrence Welk Show"), the Special Olympics and, of course food. With minimal prompting, she can recite the menu for each holiday, stating her favorites as turkey, stuffing, gravy, etc. or whatever treats she associates with the event. She delights in the company around her, but equally enjoys her solitary time. She's clearly the *one in charge* and rightly usually gets her wish. She has little concept of politics, world events or fiscal matters. She does, however, understand the concepts of pain, joy, anger, right and wrong as well as beauty. My statements are based solely on my experience of a dear sibling and could probably be enlightened or even challenged by professional thought. I choose to believe that she is as I described in Chapter 2, *Insecurity*, selected for whatever reason to lead the life she does, with overall innocence and trust.

What would it be like to trust in a non-judgmental or non-pre-conceived manner and to approach our interactions with innocence? Perhaps naiveté drives this thought, but consider a world as such . . . one where we do not even question motivation, action or thought, one where we act independently but depend upon others for sustenance, enrichment and a whole sense of self?

THERE'S NO ROOM FOR OPPRESSION

*Let every one of us please **his** neighbor for **his** good to edification.*
- Romans 15:2, The Holy Bible, King James Version -

OPPRESSION EXISTS OMNIPRESENTLY, IN VARYING degrees and manifestations. Whether it be societal, economic, belief, or authoritarian, I would imagine that most if not all of us have experienced some sort of oppression.

A quick glance at Wikipedia[3] under this topic lists the following types of societal oppression (also mentioned are two from the above, authoritarian and "socio"economic):

---

[3] <u>https://en.wikipedia.org/wiki/Oppression</u> (2020)

Privilege	Racial	Class	Gender
Sexuality	Religious	Age	Domination
Institutional	Economic	Feminism	Equal rights

Let's take a bit of a different look at a few of the above as we've discussed poverty and, to some degree, authoritarianism previously.

With respect to age oppression, what can be stated that has not already been reported, commented about or known generally? Have you ever come across an elderly person who just cannot seem to *just move it along?* Whether in the market, a parking lot of a retail outlet or any other venue, I would imagine that many of us have experienced the lack of patience one feels, particularly in this day and age when all around us moves at such an accelerated rate. Here is an example that is somewhat *opposite* in nature: a few years ago, we purchased a new vehicle, specifically bought in anticipation of the typical East Coast winter weather and snowstorms that occur. This vehicle was the largest that I had ever driven, and while not one of those "monster" SUVs, it was large for me. I had some difficulty with backing out of parking spaces, despite the luxury of having a rearview camera. I recall being at the drug store one day, shortly after buying this car, and slowly backing out from my parking space, perfectly able to see directly behind me, thanks to the camera, but really unable to see to the rear left and right of me to determine if there were

There's No Room (for) ...

any oncoming cars. I glanced to my left to see quite the elderly gentleman gesticulating at me with seemingly disgusted motions. My window was up, so I was not able to discern his statements, but I imagine they may have been laced with expletives and flavored with a demand for me to 'hurry the *** up' and move along. I felt two reactions in the moment. First, I felt somewhat ashamed. Ashamed that I was not yet comfortable enough with this new SUV to be more expedient in my reversing, but also ashamed that I was being maligned (read *oppressed*) by another, clearly of much greater age than I (as many of us no doubt feel and believe, do we not feel that we are the same person at the age of 40 or 50 as we did at the age of 20 or 30? Aside from the occasional ache or pain, or slight lapse in memory, do not most of us at least like to believe that we are still the vibrant, active and healthy beings that we've been all of our lives?). Secondly, I felt angry. Although the thought was fleeting, I recall wanting to roll down the window and engage with this gentleman, perhaps saying something to the likes of 'what are you in such a hurry for and where could you possibly need to be next that you can't wait a *** minute for me to back up, you old codger.' Thankfully, I did not act upon that fleeting thought, although, in hindsight, as I share this now, the thought and recollection of this interaction has stayed with me.

Now, I realize that the above anecdote is probably far from the most direct interpretation of oppression. However, I share this from my own perspective, and I must state that I did feel a bit oppressed, if in no other way than in spirit, internal thought and a thoughtful reflection upon my cognitive reactions. Age oppression works both ways. I often ponder what may have occurred had I acted upon my feelings of anger. Would an altercation have resulted in a worse outcome, whether verbal, physical or otherwise? Would I have gained anything from acting? I choose to believe that I would not. I drove away, feeling a bit sad.

I've touched on the topic of oppression in several of the earlier chapters: racial, religious, ethnic, etc. However, I'd like to further reflect upon my thoughts about the causes of oppression and oppressive behavior, often resulting in negative outcomes, not the least of which being mass death or destruction.

What drives one to hate another? I doubt that many broad actions of a civil or non-civil nature are driven by a personal relationship founded in mutual hate, for whatever reason. Could it be that one group's beliefs encourage or espouse intolerance, and by extension, potential violence, against another group? Could it be that the disparities discussed earlier (economic, societal, civil or human rights based, etc.) drive hate and potentially nefarious actions against another group? Or is it the often innate need to feel a part of something greater than self? That is, we often see individuals gathered for whatever reason, taking whatever action they feel is deemed appropriate, while garnering larger numbers as the action progresses. Or, and finally, is there some genetic quality, or

There's No Room (for) . . .

influence of others during youth (from family, peers or others) that leads many of us to feel that we are either *less than*, have less or are not as worthy as others?

I believe we all have the right to our own opinions, beliefs, values and actions. However, at what point do any of these morph into an action that may be deleterious to others?

Perhaps the more appropriate title to this work should have been "There's No Room for Oppression" and I could have written each sub-section from that launching point. However, I choose to call out this topic separately as I believe and hope that it may cause quiet contemplative thought.

There's No Room for Hopelessness

*But the God of all grace, who hath called us unto his eternal glory by Christ Jesus, after that ye have suffered a while, make you perfect, establish, strengthen, settle **you**.*
- 1 Peter 5:10, The Holy Bible, King James Version -

This short chapter caps off this small work with a hope for our future.

Much of what I have written has been negative, or at least some of the experiences shared are, at best, sad. I offer that we, as individuals, communities, families and even nations, have much for which to be hopeful.

We see acts of kindness and selflessness all around us, almost on a daily if not on a more frequent basis. The person who holds the door for you. The simple thank you note for a gift or gesture. The volunteerism that many of us complete to support those less fortunate. The sharing of a homemade food or homegrown flowers with others.

More broadly, we witness the acts of individuals, corporations, non-profit organizations and the like who devote funds, talents and actions for any number of worthy causes. Even our governmental institutions are structured in some measure to support our population (I recognize that this statement may be fraught with conflict of thought, but I felt it important to acknowledge).

Perhaps the most meaningful gestures of hope, at least for me personally, are found in the personal interactions I regularly experience. The brief, yet tender touch on my shoulder or torso from Wayne as we pass each other on our way to our various tasks. The kind words and expressions of love that I receive daily from my parents and often from those in the community I discussed earlier. Or just those rare moments that I spend looking out of my upstairs dormer window, from where I have written this, and pausing to marvel at the world I see: a world of vibrant growth of woods and foliage, a world of passersby on their way to work or other tasks, a world of beauty, all intended for us each to enjoy and appreciate in our own ways. A world that sometimes teeters on survival, but a world that, with hope, can continue to offer all of the good things we need and appreciate but also a world that can be even better. All with effort, empathy, compassion and, perhaps most importantly, hope.

There's No Room (for) ...

Susan personifies the hope concept. She is rarely, if ever, in a foul mood (other than when awaiting the arrival of her chicken nuggets). While not able to express *hope*, all who know her realize the impact that she brings: a gentle demeanor, a selfless and non-judgmental affect and a visceral spirit of hope, inspiring each person she may encounter. How we might cherish the innocence of her being and the love that she displays, albeit in her own way, to the world around her.

Finally, I find that hope comes from within, at least for me. While I imagine that we all wrestle with the conflicting thoughts of despair vs. hope, I am trying my best to think and act in a hopeful manner. We have very little control over the events that occur around us, and perhaps it's helpful to remember that as we march through our daily lives, often witnessing or hearing of atrocities of whatever measure, size or impact, that we remember that: we are often not in control. However, I am compelled to posit that we do have the ability to manage our thoughts, emotions, reactions and actions.

Epilogue

There's No Room (for) . . ., as described at the beginning, was written with pure intent to help us all to reflect upon our actions, values, beliefs and thoughts. There is no judgement intended in any anecdote that I've shared. There is no prescriptive direction implied or meant to be inferred. There is no example shared that should inspire any of us to act in any way that is detrimental to any member of our society.

Rather, the intent of this small work is to hopefully ameliorate the manner in which we interact with one another, as humans residing on a planet that is teetering in many ways: climatic, political, societal and many others. The hope is and has always been that the expression of these words reminds us all that our lives here are precious, passing us by with unmarked acceleration and of value to whatever creator in which you may believe, to each other and to the forwarding of progress in this world.

I have related several experiences that are of a personal nature. I pray that each of these will not offend, but, rather, offer a glimpse into the personal thoughts (and actions) of a flawed person, as I would believe that we all are, to some degree, far from perfect. I strive to be a better resident, partner, family member and contributor; but it's just that: a challenging goal.

May each of you who read this narrative experience the joy that each day brings, the happiness that is meant for us to enjoy and the knowledge that there really is no room for being anything other than what you are. We are a part of a bigger puzzle, a vital and sustaining member of our world community and we lend our values, talents and gifts without regret, hesitance or selfishness. I take no effrontery in saluting our humanity while condemning injustice. Rather, I recognize that life is a journey, one that presents challenges and rewards, one that celebrates the great times and sadly mourns the hard times and one that for which I believe we should ultimately be grateful.

I humbly thank you for reading this work and hope, as mentioned at the start, that a small snippet may resonate for you. It is with a sincere wish for a multitude of blessings for you that I conclude.

There's No Room (for) ...

My Purpose

By Jill Gallina

What is the meaning of this life that I've been given?
What is the reason for it all?
Will there be challenges, new pathways to be driven?
What is my purpose and my call?
No one can know if fame and fortune lies before me, or if my name will be unknown.
But still someday, someway I hope to make a difference.
Just by the kindnesses I've shown.
And may I be the best that I can be, and live each day with grace, and dignity! And treat others as I hope that they'd treat me, lovingly!
And may I live a life worth living.
One for loving and for giving.
Yes, this must be my purpose and my call!
And may I always hear the music in it all!

What is the meaning of this path of life I've traveled?
What is my purpose and my call?
I can't help wondering as each new day has unraveled, what is the reason for it all?
If I could choose two words to live by every day there are two words that come to mind.
When others speak of me I hope that they would say . . . that I was good and I was kind!
And may I be the best that I can be, and live each day with grace, and dignity! And treat others as I hope that they'd treat me, lovingly!
And may I live a life worth living.
One for loving and for giving.
Yes this must be my purpose and my call!
And may I always hear the music, the sweet and gentle music, may I always hear the music in it all![4]

---

[4] "My Purpose," words and music by Jill Gallina, www.jillandmichaelgallina.com Copyright: 2018 GallinaMusic LL